T0132302

SUBTLE ISN'T MY STYLE . . .

Tales from an Unfiltered Yenta (Busybody)

NIELI LANGER

Order this book online at www.trafford.com
or email orders@trafford.com

Most Trafford titles are also available at major online book retailers.

 www.trafford.com

North America & international
toll-free: 844 688 6899 (USA & Canada)
fax: 812 355 4082

Our mission is to efficiently provide the world's finest, most comprehensive book publishing service, enabling every author to experience success. To find out how to publish your book, your way, and have it available worldwide, visit us online at www.trafford.com

Because of the dynamic nature of the Internet, any web addresses or links contained in this book may have changed since publication and may no longer be valid. The views expressed in this work are solely those of the author and do not necessarily reflect the views of the publisher, and the publisher hereby disclaims any responsibility for them.

Any people depicted in stock imagery provided by Getty Images are models, and such images are being used for illustrative purposes only.
Certain stock imagery © Getty Images.

ISBN: 978-1-6987-1599-5 (hc)
ISBN: 978-1-6987-1597-1 (sc)
ISBN: 978-1-6987-1598-8 (e)

Library of Congress Control Number: 2023922860

Print information available on the last page.

Trafford rev. 12/05/2023

Dedication

This book is dedicated to my team of specials:
Daniel, Maya, Madelyn, Alexis, Noah, Remy, Harry

It has become popular to quote Dr. Seuss' book, "Oh the Places You'll Go" at graduations and at rites of passage. It's true, you all have 'brains in your head and feet in your shoes; you can steer yourself in any direction you choose.' However, I prefer to quote Julia Roberts from the movie, "Pretty Woman." She encourages her friend, Kit, a hooker, to attend beauty school. She tells Kit that she has 'potential.' I'm not Julia Roberts and I have my own recommendations for you:

People should not walk in the footsteps of others. They should create their own footsteps and march to the beat of their own drum.

Grandparents are there
to help the child
get into mischief they
haven't thought of yet.
—GENE PERRET

TABLE OF CONTENTS

Nazenti Store
(as advertised on
Amazon)

Introduction

The art of storytelling evolved naturally because some people prefer telling tales while others prefer listening to them.

Once upon a time, Truth went about the streets as naked as the day she was born. As a result, Truth, naked and cold, had been turned away from every door in the village; nobody would let her into their homes. One day, when Truth was huddled in a corner, shivering and hungry, Parable sought her out. Now, Parable was dressed in splendid clothes of beautiful colors. Parable said, "Tell me, neighbor, what makes you look so sad?" Truth replied bitterly, "Ah, brother; things are bad; very bad. I'm old, very old, and no one wants to acknowledge me. No one wants anything to do with me." Hearing that, Parable took pity on her, gathered her up and took her home. "Let me lend you some splendid clothes like mine and you'll see that the very people who pushed you aside will invite you into their homes and be glad of your company." Then, Parable dressed Truth in story, warmed her and sent her out again. Clothed in story, Truth knocked again at the villagers' doors and was readily welcomed into their homes. They invited her to eat at their table and warm herself by their fire. (Rabbi Jacob Kranz, 18" century)

I have learned that clothing truth in story is a powerful way to get people to open the doors of their minds and hearts to the message I was trying to convey. Telling stories has always been the "hook" behind my more than 45 years in the classroom at all grade levels. From young children to doctoral students, everyone listens to an idea if it is clothed in story. What I have written here are my "truths" and, therefore, my stories. Life usually tells the best stories.

My Grandchildren Stand on the Shoulders of "Giants"

In the Jewish faith, there is the legend of the Lamed Vov, unknown 36 virtuous men who hold the fate of the world in their hands. No one knows who they are, not even they.

Saba (grandfather) Menachem, an educator, emigrated to British Palestine in the 1930's. In an effort to forestall Jewish immigration into British mandated Palestine after WWII, the British established internment camps on the island of Cyprus. Menachem was smuggled onto the island in order to establish a school system for the detainees' children. At the conclusion of WWII, he was sent by the newly established State of Israel to "buy back" Jewish children from churches and monasteries where they had been placed by parents fearing their offsprings' extermination. He brought back hundreds of orphans to Israel.

Saba Joe was interned in Buchenwald Concentration Camp, outside of Berlin. To facilitate their own tasks, the Nazis introduced what was called "self-administration." The system placed a portion of camp organization and authoritarian responsibility on select prisoners who were called "kapos." Unless prisoners of upright character occupied the various camp posts (which was rare), it added further indignities to the lives of ordinary prisoners.

"What do you say, Jew? You have been selected to be a camp kapo." Saba Joe lunged at the officer and grabbed him by the neck with one hand while repeatedly pummeling him in the face with his other fist. However, before Saba Joe had the opportunity to inflict more serious damage, several guards beat him repeatedly over the head until he passed out. He was dragged into the barracks and was lucky not to have been shot. However, for the rest of his life, he suffered involuntary and rhythmic shaking of his head. He was often chastised by people who thought he was indicating "no" before they finished speaking. He always had to explain the shaking was involuntary.

Saba Joe refused to perpetrate an injustice by becoming a camp guard even if it meant potentially saving himself. Both Menachem and Joe were courageous and just men. My grandchildren are proud to claim their names.

Grandson's Tattoo of Saba Joe's date of liberation from Buchenwald Concentration Camp, April 11, 1945 . . .

Lessons from My Father, Joe

My father was a great teacher; he was my role model. He taught me to never underestimate myself; he said Jews have to swim faster…they have shorter arms! When we went to see the Rockettes at Radio City Music Hall, he never went to the end of the line that snaked around 6th Avenue. Joe planted himself close to the box office and when people made comments or the ushers urged him to move, he simply said, "No speak English."

He introduced me to the cinema, to the opera and the theater. His love and appreciation of what New York had to offer to new immigrants was infectious and I became convinced, till this day, that New York is the capital/center of the universe.

Joe was also creative and whenever I had a school project, he would drool in anticipation of partnering with me in its execution. When I needed a science project, we decided (or maybe he did) that we were going to make a model of the human brain. He brought home the head of a large bald doll and took me to the shoemaker where he purchased wax to melt over the head. The soft wax enabled me to carve all the sections into a reasonable facsimile of the human brain. The success of the project was not only the grade, but I learned to become resourceful in organizing and executing projects.

Joe also explained the following: we were slaves in Egypt, we were deported to Babylon, we were second class citizens under Rome and the Nazis sought to annihilate us…We're Still Standing.

You do what the Jews have always done…you hang on! And, when you live amongst non-Jews, you go out of your way to make sure that you do not cast shame upon the Jewish people by your individual actions.

Nieli . . . free to be me

This collection of tales, guarded advice and personal observations during a life well-lived, is also dedicated to my father, Joe Lieberman. This book represents a collection of stories, guarded advice and personal observations during a life well-lived. There wasn't a day when he didn't crack a bawdy joke, tell a timely tale or share an important life lesson. He instilled confidence and taught me that money and power cannot compare with being an honorable and generous human being. Every day after school he would ask me if I had been a "mensch" (respectful person) that day. If he is watching from above, he might very well accept my roadmap for life, "do no harm, but take no shit."

Aren't <u>genes</u> something to smile about???

Saba Joe and his great grandson . . .

My Advisor on Political Correctness

To Be or Not to Be . . .

The scene was set, the stagehands ready; then, with impeccable dramatic timing, the starlet arrived and took center stage for her premier performance of Susie Snowflakes.

No one wanted to see her daughter on Broadway more than my mother, Ella Lieberman. She dismissed the fact that I was no beauty and could hardly carry a tune. However, this night was going to go down in history as Nieli's debut at the Brooklyn Paramount Theater.

Just as I started singing, " Here comes Susie Snowflakes," Ella was so overcome with joy and anticipation, that she passed out in the aisle! She never saw my debut. However, when the audience clamored for an encore, the revived Ella lost her cool AGAIN and passed out for the second time.

Needless to say, Nieli would have to become a star in a different venue, OFF STAGE!

Morality Tale

A little bird was flying south for the winter. It got so cold it froze up and fell to the ground. While it was lying there, a cow came by and dropped some dung on it. As it lay there, the bird began to realize how warm it was.

Warm and snug, he soon began to sing for joy. A passing cat heard the singing and came to investigate. The cat discovered the bird under the cow dung and promptly dug him out and ate him up!

The moral of the story:

1. Not everyone who shits on you is your enemy
2. Not everyone who gets you out of shit is your friend.
3. When you are in deep shit, keep your mouth shut.

When Omission Derails a Mission…

Hanna and Paul were engaged to be married. They were also what has been termed "trophy children," the progeny of Holocaust survivors whose children had been murdered by the Nazis in concentration camps. As such, they were raised by parents who had great aspirations for their children's success. One major goal was graduation from an American university. Both Hanna and Paul anticipated graduation a few weeks before the upcoming wedding.

One evening, a few weeks before the commencement of both events, Paul called Hanna and related the following: "You know how we both anticipated our graduations? Well, I won't be graduating; I don't have enough credits."

Hanna was stunned. Considering what she assumed was their mutual values, she was not only shocked but sickened by Paul's admission. Intellectually, she could comprehend the postponement of his graduation. But, what she now questioned was, who was she really marrying? What other surprises awaited her after they took their vows?

Many of you might see Paul's omission as trivial and Hanna's reaction an overreaction; others would question Hanna's lack of trust and loyalty to Paul and their commitment to one another. Needless to say, Hanna no longer had faith in Paul and that weekend she broke their engagement.

If you have an alternative reaction or would like to comment on this real-life scenario, please contact the author at ninilanger@gmail.com.

I would like to hear from you…

Nieli and Neil...

When Harry Met Sally set a new standard for romantic comedies. In *An Officer and a Gentleman, the* Navy makes Richard Gere an officer, but the love of a good woman, Debra Winger, reveals his inner gentleman. The underlying theme of *Nieli and Neil* has no romantic or comedic elements. Neil doesn't even know that Nieli exists! However, Nieli has consistently been devoted to Neil and all his endeavors.

Neil Diamond was born in Brighton Beach, Brooklyn, to Jewish immigrants from Poland. My folks, also Polish immigrants, moved to an apartment a few blocks from Neil's childhood home. His father owned a dry-goods store not far from my parents' apartment. This is when our "relationship" commenced! Although we both attended Lincoln High, we never met. However, it was my mother who initiated the relationship i.e., she used to buy my underwear from his father's dry goods store!

All underwear aside, I developed an intuitive appreciation for his music, ever since he recorded "Solitary Man" and "Cherry, Cherry." Filling a musical void that existed between Frank Sinatra and Elvis Presley, Neil found wide acceptance among all generations.

Aware of his lack of acting talent, Neil performed only in one major movie, the remake of The Jazz Singer. Despite the almost universally negative reviews of the film, it grossed 3 times its budget. Neil's hit single, "America" which was part of the soundtrack, resounded when the hostages came back from Iran in 1981.

The essence of my regard for Neil is that his voice is honest and soulful. His unique style combined with his powerful stage presence, has made him such a likeable performer. When he sings, he is not singing for you; it is as if he and you were there to do something together.

I Was Your Teacher

I have been many people in many places, i.e., Israel, South Africa, Texas, New York, and currently Knoxville, Tennessee. Throughout the course of my teaching duties, I have been called upon to be friend, coach, psychologist, and advocate.

The names of those who have practiced my profession are wide-ranging and encompass the best minds in history . . . Confucius, Moses, Jesus, Helen Keller, Socrates . . . I am also those people whose names have been forgotten but whose lessons and character will be remembered in the accomplishments of their students.

My greatest gifts were in what I was willing to receive from my students AND as a seeker of new opportunities for my students from elementary school through doctoral studies in gerontology and social work.

I have in my teaching career fought peer pressure, prejudice, and ignorance. But I have had great allies: your intelligence, curiosity, creativity, love and laughter. You attended my classes and taught me as much as I taught you. As such, I have a past that is rich in memories. I wish each of you what you wish for yourselves.

My Holocaust (Amir Gutfreund)

Reviewed By: Annette M. Hintenach, PhD;
(2018) revised by N. Langer
Fordham University Graduate School of
Social Service, New York, NY

The book features two friends, Amir and Effi who live in Haifa, Israel; they strive to learn as much as they can about what happened "over there." They are repeatedly rebuffed by their parents, older residents, and survivors with a dismissive, 'you are not old enough to understand the events' which further fuels their desire for answers.

Amir and Effi have very few "real" relatives aside from their own parents; as a result, they designate older friends and neighbors as their surrogate grandparents. This system of assigning familial titles, i.e., grandpa or even uncle, to otherwise non-family acquaintances, helped to create a familial social support network that had been erased by the events of the Holocaust.

The two friends are surrounded by an eclectic and extensive cast of characters as they move from childhood to adulthood. Life for them is profoundly shaped by Grandpas Lolek and Yosef. Grandpa Lolek is a stingy curmudgeon who fought the Nazis in World War II as a soldier in the Polish cavalry and whose family perished in the gas chambers. Grandpa Yosef is his exact opposite. He is regarded as the neighborhood saint, wise and all-knowing, who is always willing to give a helping hand, yet adamantly refusing to speak of his own haunted past.

As the friends mature, they remain relentless in their pursuit of knowledge about the Shoah. They turn to numerous "relatives" for information and are repeatedly rebuffed for not being 'old enough'. When the two lifelong friends become older, Amir's need to learn more about the Shoah turns into an obsession. He begins to fastidiously chronicle the many heartbreaking and gut-wrenching stories about the past as recited by his own father, bolstered by events described by his surrogate survivor grandfathers and neighbors. As more and more individuals share their stories, the two friends are lost about how to handle this horrendous information. Their reactions are pure and raw.

These revelations give the reader a glimpse of the environments in which the children of survivors were raised and the trauma of living and being raised by often depressed and sometimes angry souls.

"Law of Compression," as described in the novel, was a collection of replacement relatives from the neighborhood. By adopting grandparents, uncles, cousins, and other relatives, survivors created familial supports that had been abruptly removed by the events of the Holocaust. The book ultimately emphasizes the need for family and family supports in our lives; when we lose these structures, we seek appropriate substitutes. In addition, the book places great emphasis on the importance of older family members as role models who hold families together and convey collective traditions and values for younger generations.

Comments . . .

I am the only daughter of Holocaust survivors who immigrated to America in 1947. The book captured the shared burden of survivors and their offspring. 'Collecting' older survivors and making them surrogate family was also part of my childhood. Like the boys' surrogate grandfathers, most survivors did not share their stories, often because of the pain in retelling and also from survivor guilt. Therefore, almost all of what I know of the Holocaust I have gleaned from books and films. Although many survivors protected their children from the horrors of their past, we children were raised by 'damaged souls." We were also trophy children who were expected to succeed as a way of honoring all those who had perished and to remind the world that Hitler hadn't succeeded in his mission to eradicate the Jews.

For Those Who Are Worthy . . .

In an upscale neighborhood in any of our 50 States, Mr. and Mrs. Chic lived with their young daughter, with the addition of Mrs. Chic's elderly mother, named Silence. At mealtime, the 3 Chic's sat down to their meal at the dining room table. Mrs. Silence had her own small table in the corner of the room facing the wall. She ate her meal in silence because she was never permitted to ask or comment on any topic of conversation. Mr. and Mrs. Chic were fearful that Mrs. Silence might utter an "inappropriate" word or allude to a comment or topic from her generation's discourse that might "upset" the family.

One day, Mrs. Chic observed that her daughter was arranging a table and chair in a corner for her doll. When Mrs. Chic asked her what she was doing, the younger Chic cheerfully responded, "I am practicing placing you in a silent corner when I grow up and you live with me!"

If Mrs. Chic was surprised or even appalled, she has her own behavior and negative attitude toward Mrs. Silence to blame for her daughter's learned actions and attitude (adapted from the Brothers Grimm). In the world in which most of us were raised, intellectual/academic achievement was the goal in most aspiring families. Emotional intelligence, more recently coined and researched, includes body language, communication skills and even facial expressions. Most parents assumed that the positive values of respect for others' feelings and opinions as well as generosity of spirit would automatically go hand in hand with the professional aspirations of their offspring. However, as depicted in the above tale, intellectual achievement has led to arrogance and has eroded any and all the values learned in their childhood, especially respect.

Respect is rooted in the idea of equality, being respectful in outward, visible ways, e.g., giving someone your full attention when they are talking — is a signal that you regard them as a peer. Encouraging different, intellectually sound opinions is the basis for the exploration of ideas. As traditional standards of speech and conduct disappear from public and private lives, the need for them has never been clearer.

To My Husband of 52 Years
Who Married Me Because I Could Type . . .

YES, ours was a teenage summer romance—two people from different worlds with common roots and values who found one another because someone else was called away . . .

YES, we battled stubborn parents, the miles that separated us and even conventional wisdom (the simple, convenient, comfortable, though not necessarily true path), in order to find one another again.

And, I said YES to the romantic marriage proposal that has gone down in family lore as the rival to a Shakespearean love sonnet . . ."So, what you 'think?' Yes, No!? . . . We waste already enough time . . ."

YES, I said because I believed that some miracle had brought us two together. We lived this miracle every day for 52 years. Of course, much of this miracle can be credited to the very useful skill that I learned in junior high school, i.e., typing. For 52 years, we brainstormed in English and Hebrew, knocked out 1 medical, 1 master's, 2 doctoral degrees, 6 books, and hundreds of professional research papers and essays.

Weather Systems (Barbara Crooker)

Sugar maples, little fires in the trees, every blazing gradation. Of orange to red, and this makes me think of you, the way you press the long length of your body against me, the heat seeping through the flannel, my own private furnace. If only hands and feet had a color, it would be blue. From November until May, I cannot get warm. Even my bones have cores of ice. But you are a house on fire, an internal combustion system, Siracha sauce/jalapeno poppers/ Thai curry. I stay up late, read until you're asleep, so I can slip my icy feet, frozen toes, under the smoldering log of your torso. Even in the dark, you radiate. 1 am a cold front, a polar low coming down from the Arctic. And you, why you, you're the sun.

Les Fauves, 2018

Marriage: Growing Older Together

And they lived happily ever after . . . What was their marriage like? As the years passed, did the prince undergo a mid-life crisis and the princess a hysterectomy? Did she decide to color her golden hair and he to take up jogging along the palace walls?

OR

Did she want no one but him? And did they spend their days walking hand in hand in the palace gardens waiting for sunset? (Silverston & Hyman, 1992)

Khalil Gibran's passage (On Marriage from the Prophet; Knopf, New York, 1923) describes that the above alternative scenarios are perhaps two parts of the same evolving marriage:

> Give your heart, but not into each other's keeping.
> For only the hand of Life can contain your hearts.
> And stand together, yet not too near together,
> For the pillars of the temple stand apart,
> And the oak tree and the cypress
> Grow not in each other's shadow.

Older couples are often less lonely and financially more stable than older single persons. Today, most married couples look forward to the post parenting years as opportunities for increased closeness. The couple relationship is a source of great comfort and support.

'Love is a Many Splendid Thing' . . . even unto illness: The Caregiver Wife

Langer, N. 2018
Educational Gerontology 44 (12):741-42

(This editorial is solely dedicated to the couple whose love has sustained them over time) . . . NLanger

Perhaps nothing will test a marriage more sorely than when a husband develops a chronic, long-term illness or disability. When two people marry, they expect to share the responsibilities of life, to communicate with each other on the deepest levels, and to give and receive love. If the wife has suddenly been put into the role of caregiver, what should she do—and how can she stay strong while she does it? Being the caregiver is a job that often comes with its own unique set of challenges. Sometimes it feels like a privilege; sometimes it feels like a burden. Sometimes it feels like both of these things, all at once. As a wife caregiver, she will be expected to fulfill many of these roles: nurse, spiritual adviser, housekeeper, accountant, chef, social director, chauffer, and lover.

In this new chapter of a couple's life, a major component, in order to navigate current and future development of events, will be the acquisition for both the husband and wife of as much knowledge of the illness and prognosis. They need to prioritize their questions—putting the most important ones first—to be sure they receive the info they need. The ill husband may or may not want complete information because for some, denial helps. However, the wife will cope better when she has accurate, firsthand information about his condition, treatment, and needs.

A wife's attitude is critical to staying positive through a tumultuous time. Even though some couples may rail against God, it is self-defeating. Both partners must try to avoid dwelling on the 'whys' and concentrate on the 'hows' to make this new chapter in the marriage livable. A major medical diagnosis can lead to doctor-recommended changes in the husband's diet, physical activity level, medication routine and need for rest. A well spouse's risk support and encouragement can help a partner stay on track, but this new role can also trigger frustration on both sides. The wife may feel anxious to get it right, relying on medical advice that has promised to place the sick spouse back on track. The ill spouse might not be used to being told what to do and feel he is being nagged. Listening more and talking less during stressful times may sidestep many confrontations. Not always sure what to say?

That's okay. The husband needs to hear that he is loved and supported, mentally and even intimately. Listening when he wants to talk, or just spending quiet time together may often be what is needed. If possible, keeping shared routines that have been part of a couple's life together—a TV movie and popcorn on Friday night, morning coffee and the daily newspaper, and/or walking the dog may provide the emotional stability that avoids the stress of the illness. After a serious diagnosis, both partners may cherish these everyday traditions more than ever.

The wife should never underestimate her needs when her partner faces a serious illness. Research involving heart-attack survivors and their partners has revealed that a well spouse's risk of depression and anxiety increases when her partner experiences a major health crisis. Researchers have found that emotional distress increases equally in both partners, yet the well spouse is less likely to receive emotional support just when she needs the strength to care for a partner in new ways. She needs to talk about her fears, frustrations and worries with someone she trusts. In addition to addressing her own health needs, she must continue with the social activities that gave her pleasure prior to her husband's diagnosis. She will feel better, resent her husband less, and be more able to support her partner.

Belonging for an older couple signifies identification as a couple, sharing of values, comfortable interaction, and a sense of safety and security. To whatever extent the caregiver wife can take the lead during this trying time, she will probably never regret being the one who found the strength, courage, and compassion to do what needed to be done.

Love and Sex: Are we ever too old?!?

By Nieli Langer, reviewed by Anne Wyat-Brown; University of Florida, Gainesville, FL. Educational Gerontology, 2018, Vol.44, 672-673.

Love and Sex sets out to reach a broad audience of "adult children, grandchildren and the current cohorts of aging individuals to understand and accept the sexuality of maturing adults," the back cover of the book claims. Nieli Langer has a PhD in social work with a specialization in gerontology. She writes as an enthusiast for the long-term sexual lives of older adults, despite the difficulties many may face from their families and the staff of their institutions, some of whom are offended by the notion that older people should have active sex lives.

As Langer herself reports further on the back cover, her book includes "a collage of photos of older couples, cartoons, selected poetry about sexuality and couplehood as well as reviews of books and films that have celebrated late-life love and sexuality." I found the poems to be touching and often funny. I enjoyed them thoroughly. The reviews of books were very short, but the books themselves were impressive. They included Erich Fromm, The Art of Loving, Gabriel Marcia Marquez, Love in the Time of Cholera, Alfred Kinsey's groundbreaking studies of the sexual behavior of men and women, as well as Alex Comfort, The Joy of Sex. Naturally, Langer did not write very much about each work in her short book, but including such references enhanced her argument.

Some years before I had read the book, I had heard that a friend of my sister-in-law, who was living in a CCRC, much like mine, had formed an attachment to another resident. Unfortunately, her children asked the staff to make sure that she and the male companion never entered her apartment together. Both my sister-in-law and I agreed that it was most unfair of her children to make that request, but of course our opinion would have been of no interest to those who ran the place. If we had known about Love and Sex, it might have been possible to have asked the children to read it, but it might have taken more than one book to have changed their minds.

I particularly liked the poems Langer selected. Some showed a real sense of humor, including one written by Judith Viorst to a husband who dumped the friend of the poet for a younger woman (69-70). Lois Wyse, a poet with whom I was also unfamiliar, had several poems that amused and touched me.

Nieli Langer, however, holds out hope that the Baby Boomer generation, younger than ours, may have more enlightened attitudes toward sex for the aged and occasionally be in favor of sexual activity even for those with dementia. If members of that generation read her book and spend time observing the behavior of men and women in such institutions, they may end by agreeing with her that maintaining an active sex life can enhance the later years of elders. From what I have observed at my CCRC, having a companion can make the later life of residents much more pleasant than it would be if they had no close relationship.

Unfortunately, a recent conversation with a friend who lives in my CCRC, alerted me to the problem of convincing the people who run nursing home facilities to allow men and women to be alone in the same bedroom. I was telling a friend about Nieli Langer's book, and her idea that sex was very important for older people. My friend told me that a couple who we all know who live in our CCRC are not permitted to be in the same apartment together. I asked why, and my friend said that the authorities in charge feared a lawsuit. This suggests that people who live in institutions may not have the same freedom as people who live in their own dwelling.

The only hope for future freedom for residents is a change of attitude on the part of the residents' families. If in the future younger family members become convinced of the benefits that relatives may experience, they may be able to reassure the people who run institutions that they will not be filing a lawsuit if their relative starts having sex with another resident. Until such time, Langer's hope for sexual freedom for residents will be a dream, not a realty.

About His Retirement

He's pointing out where I left some dust on the baseboards.
He's watching out for which foods I am letting go bad.
He's giving me guidance on how to water the houseplants.
He says that I ought to be glad. I am not glad.

He's nudging me when I fail to floss after mealtime.
He's alerting me when I gain even half a pound.
He's pestering me to straighten my spine and stop slouching
whenever he's around. He is always around.

He's starting conversations with me when I'm reading.
He's chiming in when I talk with my friends on the phone.
He's coming with me when I shop at the supermarket
So, I won't have to shop alone. I like alone.

He's sitting beside me while I'm tweezing my eyebrows.
He's standing beside me while I'm blow-drying my hair.
He's sharing those moments when I am clipping my toenails.
You want my opinion? He's overdoing share.

He's keeping track of how I am spending each second.
He also keeps track of how much I spend on my clothes.
Before he retired I told him he must find a hobby.
Now he's retired. And guess who's the hobby he chose?"

Judith Viorst 2000

The greatest thing you'll ever learn
is just to love and be loved in return...
—Nat King Cole ("Nature Boy")[4]

What is a Widow?

In word processing, a widow is the last line of a paragraph that appears as the first line of a page. Widows are considered bad form in page layout, so many word processors allow you to avoid them. The Hebrew word for widow (*almanah*) comes from the root word *alem*, which means "unable to speak" or "mute." (Carolyn James, The Gospel of Ruth, page 62). The widow is simultaneously bad form in writing and voiceless in human relations! As a widow, you have become superfluous or an addendum.

Someone or something has hit the mute button and you are unable to articulate how you feel or what you are really thinking. Or, is anyone even listening? As a widow, you lose your voice especially with your children. Instead of 'I can, 'I will," or 'I think," you are relegated to asking 'May 1?'

If a widow is to continue to live, she will need to force herself to find a new path, a new way that is unique to her. Although the word widow has a universal definition, no two widows travel the journey of widowhood on the same road. To find her voice, or to find her way, it takes a lot of soul searching, i.e., time, energy and focus. Some widows never come to terms with this new stage in life and they rail against the gods; others slowly and sometimes painfully carve out an alternative to their previous life. When people say that time will help a widow heal to one who was once a beloved spouse cannot fathom the pain that never ceases.

Use your mind and heart and then speak what is in both. Hopefully, someone will listen. But, if they don't, you have still spoken; you are not mute. You may be a widow, but you are able to speak. Let your life speak for you and words will support it.

Two Faces Have I

Baby boomers have and will continue to have the opportunity to be parents for many years. However, no one can say the relationship between them and their adult children will always be easy. What do they complain about? What do we grumble and carp about? We are often proud and confident that we have nurtured and launched our often very successful children. However, we "walk on eggshells" as we navigate the mutual relations. There seems to be an endless cycle whereby they confide in us and then retreat; we dread their unresponsiveness and scorn, and they, in turn fear "the narrowing of our eyes" in judgment. For every heartbroken parent who wonders why their child doesn't call, there is the frustrated adult child who yearns to be acknowledged as an adult. How do we foster good relationships with our adult children? Lou Christie's 1963 hit song Two Faces Have I, although originally about a lost love, in the context of evolving parent/adult child relations, is fitting here.

Two faces have I

I don't want the world to know
I don't want my heart to show
Two faces have I
I pretend that I am happy
But I'm Mr. Blue
I pretend that I am happy
Since I lost you
Two faces have I
One to laugh and one to cry (Roulette Records, 1963)

The challenge becomes how to find common ground without overstepping the comfortable boundaries between you. How much information should you share? Which battles should you fight and when should you retreat? How much unsolicited and often underappreciated advice should you offer? We need to acknowledge at how well our grown-up offspring have navigated parenthood. Our children need us to bear witness to their increasing capacity to take on responsibilities. Remember when you were #1? Step aside and allow your daughter-in-law or son-in-law to assume that place of honor.

As parents, we are in the business of putting ourselves out of a job when our children grow up. However, if we practice good listening skills, ask intelligent questions and offer alternative solutions when solicited, always keep the light on and the pocketbook slightly ajar, we may yet successfully navigate this glorious and memorable time. (Isay, J. 2008) Walking on eggshells

Your Grown Children May Not Want Your Stuff . . .

There is a kink in the chain of passing down mementoes from one generation to another in many societies. This resistance has its roots in changing aesthetic tastes. Many families can minimize the hurt feelings and angst that accompany the rejection of family heirlooms by sitting down and deciding what items will be kept by family members, donated to charity, or tossed in the dumpster.

I took pictures of each item and each grown child received a copy of the photos to be viewed, or not, at a future date. The children felt less pressure about this collective effort.

Remember, too, that your children may not cherish your collectibles but your grandchildren might prize them. Grandchildren should not be left out of the process of downsizing and distribution. Years ago, my young son wanted his great grandfather's five-n-dime wristwatch while my daughter sought her grandmother's tea towels! What we choose to keep is not always a practical endeavor but most certainly an emotional one.

The real crux of the issue is not the actual item but the memories and emotions that these items illicit for the older generation. But, for Heaven's sake, don't guilt your grown children into keeping your stuff!

Your Grandchildren May Inherit Your Wealth BUT, Will They Inherit Your Values?

Ethical wills or legacy letters are not new; they are heartfelt expressions of what truly matters most in a person's life and provide a personal message to a younger generation. Creative grandparents often play meaningful roles in their grandchildren's lives. As walking history books, many have taught valuable truths and skills that grandchildren could never have learned at school. They recited stories of family lore and some of these stories were *even* true. There is probably nothing more valuable to grandchildren than knowing that they are unconditionally loved and valued. In return, they teach us things and even program our cell phones and computers. My legacy letter articulates what I value and have incorporated into my life. I bequeath these values to my grandchildren in hopes that they may borrow them and incorporate them into their lives.

1. We were all kneaded from the same dough but we were each baked differently; respect the difference.
2. It is not where you were born; it is the values that launched and nurtured you by your family that ultimately determined who you became.
3. God gave us two ears and one mouth; listen twice as much as you speak.
4. Of course, I talk to myself . . . sometimes I need expert advice.
5. Treat others as you want to be treated. Remember, the toes that you may be stepping on today, could be attached to the ass you will be kissing tomorrow.
6. Life is too short to be serious all the time; so, if you can't laugh at yourself, just call on me, and I'll laugh at you.
7. My people skills are just fine; it's my lack of tolerance for both stupidity and arrogance that needs work.
8. The halls of justice are NOT filled with justice. Justice depends on who you know and how many zeroes you have in your bank account.

9. The shark on the right knew every dance move . . . but it was the shark on the left who went rogue and danced to his own crazy beat and stole the show. Don't ever be a conformist for convenience's sake (Meredith Vieira)

10. Sometimes the thoughts in my head get bored and go for a stroll out through my mouth; this is never a good thing . . . be mindful.

11. The greatest gift you can give someone is your undivided attention.

12. Remember, nothing is accomplished alone. We need others and very often they need us, too. You may find yourself in the role of mentor, motivator/cheerleader. Friends may often fulfill these roles for you, too.

Memories and History

Memory is the single most unifying force of human identity, and people should be the owners and interpreters of their own memories. Popular memory is how an event is remembered. That event itself could be a primary source depending on who is telling the story. History, on the other hand, is a compilation of various sources used to describe an event. Therefore, there are 2 types of history, i.e., the one that we have lived and been influenced by and the other that is our collective history most often described in books. Memory is how we remember our own history.

How often have you told a story and your grown children chime in, "Mom, that's not what really happened. You are embellishing and twisting the facts." However, we are entitled to our own memories and the way we remember and interpret the events. I even have a friend who begins to describe his involvement in an event when, in fact, he wasn't even there! When my children begin to interrupt my rendition of an event claiming, "It wasn't like that," I get angry not only at their interruption but the fact that they purport to infringe on MY memory. If they remember an event differently, let them recite their own version. Always remember that at the scene of an accident, ten witnesses will each have their own version of what transpired.

Several years ago, however, I was redeemed. When my daughter, granddaughter and I were reminiscing, my daughter told a story and at the end, her daughter chimed in with, "Mom, it didn't happen like that!" My daughter got flustered but I couldn't help grinning. I had witnessed her comeuppance! She stuttered and couldn't make eye contact with me.

Each of us sees, remembers and lives an event differently. We need to respect that and allow each version its due. Maybe several versions are correct and make family lore even richer.

Preserving and Eliciting Memories

Stories passed down through the generations leave an important legacy for families. Memories may not be spectacular, but they are an important record of our history through the decades and a source of heritage information for relatives. Senior adults may also say that what happened to them is not important, because they don't want to bore someone else with their memories. Interested relatives may need to encourage them to tell their stories because these storytellers are often about ordinary people with extraordinary lives.

Sharing memories helps older adults relive past events in their lives. By sharing memories, older adults can explore their thoughts and feelings about the past. They can put their past experiences into perspective with what is happening to them in the present or what is expected to happen in the future.

While writing or reciting may sometimes be difficult because it brings back painful memories, it may, for many looking back, bring some peace. Preserving one's memories keeps not only family and events alive, it preserves the storyteller: I am and will continue to be remembered. Storytelling can improve the confidence of older adults. By recalling how they overcame past struggles, they are better able to confront new challenges and can forgive themselves their mistakes. Their stories are often vital lessons for relatives who hear their stories, i.e., what to do and not do in their own lives.

In long term care facilities, storytelling programs, most often called life review or reminiscence by professional practitioners, have become vital care protocols. Storytelling and sharing memories is beneficial to terminally ill patients by addressing their need to feel that life has meaning and purpose. Patients often find it helpful to put their lives in perspective. When transcripts have been made of these sessions, family members of patients who had died said the transcripts consoled them while they grieved.

For practitioners, the open-ended question is the most important tool: *How are you feeling today? How many children and grandchildren do you have?* Other helpful tools include active listening, responding positively, asking follow- up questions, and allowing time for silence and emotion. These skills also require that we be curious enough and interested enough in the other person to make sure we are clear about what they are saying, asking for clarification and reflecting back to make sure we have heard correctly. It is about taking seriously that the conversation is not about us but about the other. For cognitively impaired patients, many memories spring from keepsakes, souvenirs, and photographs. Using objects as prompts for memories is especially helpful for patients with dementia. Sensory stimulation through sound, movement, dance, smell, vibration, and food can also trigger strong memories.

The Golden Rule guides people to choose for others what they would choose for themselves. It is an imperative whether the listener is a relative or a care provider. People want to be heard and, through that hearing, respected. They don't want words; they want attention and presence. Even when the relative or patient is looking for an answer, listening and creating a space for them to reflect is all they need to come to the answer themselves rather than having anyone impose it on them.

Langer, N. Educational Gerontology, 2018; Preserving and eliciting memories

Patients Have an Illness Story

Have you ever had the feeling that you are merely answering your doctor's questions and not really being heard or understood? If your answer is yes, try telling him/her your illness story. After all, that's why you came to see him/her in the first place! Storytelling is probably the best method for communicating important, sometimes difficult thoughts in a simple and memorable way. The time has come for the patient's story to take back its rightful place after having been pushed aside in the name of managed care and more efficient use of clinic visits. Care providers need to periodically refresh their knowledge of the contents of the Hippocratic Oath.

The illness is part of you, your family and culture and it can only be understood when you tell your story. Your story lets your physician into your life, look for meaning in your illness and hopefully discover ways for you to cope with it. If your physician is really listening, your story can be a very effective way for you and your physician to better understand what is actually going on.

Some patients, however, may be reluctant to tell their stories. They may feel they are 'being a burden' by unloading their problems or feel uncomfortable or embarrassed. If physicians also don't bother to ask patients to tell their stories, they may never learn important facts that could help in finding a proper diagnosis. If at all possible, the patient needs to speak directly to the physician, not through a relative, friend, or neighbor who serve as facilitators and/or interpreters. If the patient can speak directly about his/her illness to the physician, the professional can learn about the cultural background, health beliefs, and patient's ability and willingness (i.e., compliance) to partner with the care provider.

An intuitive physician will be alert to what the patient says and what he/she holds back. The patient's nods and shrugs and even body language will help support the storytelling. The physician that doesn't encourage the patient to tell his/her story is losing an important opportunity that could help him/her be a more effective health provider.

When the patient tells his/her story, the physician needs to listen and repeat what he/she thinks they have heard. Patients should be able to agree/disagree with the physician's summary of the narrative in order to make sure it is accurate. When the patient recites his/her illness story, and the physician is actually listening, a partnership is created in maximizing the patient's health care. Stories express feelings and communicate ideas that the listener needs to hear. Telling and listening to a story makes it a mutual experience.

Modern medicine needs to learn again how to combine compassion and understanding learned from a patient's story with the knowledge and honesty needed to ease patients' suffering and pain.

The Lilith Summer by Hadley Irwin

The Feminist Press at CUNY;
(reprint 1993); 128 pages

Reviewed by Danielle Jimenez
PhD Candidate
Fordham University, New York

Hadley Irwin is the pen name of Lee and Annabelle Irwin who wrote and published many books together. They have received awards from the American Library Association and the Jane Addams Peace Association for their contributions to literature that focus on issues facing teenagers and young adults. Irwin's first book, The Lilith Summer, is a fictional story that uses the relationship between two characters, 12-year-old Ellen and 77-year-old Lilith Adams, to convey two contrasting perspectives of the lived experiences of "older adults. The gap in age between the two main characters provides a useful juxtaposition of perspectives related to how the lives of older adults are interpreted. Irwin uses the dialogue and relationship between Ellen and Lilith to convey how ageist beliefs impact how older adults are perceived. Lilith's wisdom, independence, and strength negate these stereotypical beliefs. This book deviates from the standard evidence-based peer-reviewed literature related to educational gerontology. The book can serve as a tool to share with / other individuals that are new to the discourse on 'ageism' and to challenge the social constructs that perpetuate stereotypes and myths about older adults.

Ageism refers to the systemic stereotyping and discrimination against people because of their age and can be insidious in nature because of how they have been ingrained within societies that place a higher value on youth than on old age (Azulai, 2014). The issues and topics related to gerontology that are conveyed in the story parallel real-life situations and challenge ageism by humanizing various issues through the characters.

The story unfolds on a linear timeline that corresponds with the chronological themes experienced throughout the life course related to human development. The book begins with an emphasis on young Ellen who begrudgingly agrees to be a paid companion to Lilith. As the story progresses, the reader learns about loss, death, and dying. Ellen is catapulted into various circumstances that challenge her preconceived notions about old people and their lives. The topics related to aging include, but are not limited to: romantic relationships, dementia, loss, fear, loneliness, mental health, friendship, and walking the fine line between ensuring one's safety and promoting individual autonomy.

Disengagement theory proposes that decreased levels of activity and separation from society is an inevitable result of aging. However, while disengaging may apply to some older individuals, the theory fails to capture the full spectrum of older adults' late life experiences (Franklin & Tate, 2008). Lilith's character is a direct challenge to the assumptions behind that theory. Irwin deconstructs the myth that older adults are asexual through the portrayal of Lilith's relationship with Mr. Cummings. Their romantic relationship contains all the characteristics of any partnership from flirtatious exchanges to the complex social situations that prevent them from legal partnership.

One of the most salient themes covered in the book is the notion of aging in place and maintaining one's autonomy. Lilith takes Ellen to a residential care facility to visit a friend. The ensuing conversation between the two friends is a poignant example of institutionalization when it is not representative of the individual's choice or circumstances. Loss of independence as we age is again underscored by Lilith's resistance to her niece's argument that she is not capable of living independently. This stereotypical assumption is based on Lilith's age and not on concrete observations to indicate an actual need. Aging is often automatically associated with death and dying when the reality is, we can face death at any given moment. The main strength of Irwin's book is the use of Lilith's character to challenge engrained assumptions about growing old.

It is important to note that the book has its limitations especially if the intention is to use it to solely question some of the prevailing negative notions about aging. Lilith's story is only one example of what positive aging looks like. Socioeconomic status, gender, physical and cognitive abilities, sexual orientation, access to social supports, and cultural/ethnic factors also impact how we age.

Institutionalization, although reflective of how some people view care facilities, is presented with a skewed emphasis on negative attributes. This can be problematic because it discredits the existence of formal care settings and care workers devoted to improving the quality of life for residents. This unbalanced presentation of institutional facilities can elicit unwarranted tension between caregivers and care recipients when physical and/or mental health deteriorate and a residential care facility is the only option.

The underlying themes throughout the book are those that all of us may find ourselves experiencing. Although the book provides only a few examples of) how aging can be experienced, the dialogue to unravel systemic ageism should occur sooner rather than later and books such as this one can be beneficial in starting the conversation.

Azulai, A. (2014). Ageism and future cohort of elderly: Implications for social work. Journal of Social Work Values and Ethics, 11(2), 2-12.

Franklin, N. C., & Tate, C. A. (2008). Lifestyle and Successful Aging: An Overview. American Journal of Lifestyle Medicine, 3(1), 6-11. doi:10.1177/ 1559827608326125

Comments...

A story is able to capture concepts that are often difficult to explain in academic, scientific language as the reviewer explained. Good narratives can evoke emotions that create connections in the mind that statistics, charts, clinical diagnoses, and figures cannot.

Every morning in Africa, a gazelle wakes up. It knows it must outrun the fastest lion or be killed. Every morning in Africa, a lion wakes up.

It knows it must run faster than the / slowest gazelle or it will starve. So, it doesn't really matter whether you're the lion or the gazelle — when the sun comes up, start running!!! (Austin, 1996, p.14)

Recounting this story is the way one general manager at Nordstrom reminds her staffers to stay on their toes. While having facts and analysis to back up your case is necessary, statistics, clinical test results, and cold hard logic mean nothing to most people. None of those things tell why you really believe something. Narratives include an emotional dimension — that is, it is not just about what happens but how the characters feel about it. People do not connect to statistics or even facts; they connect to emotions, personalities and the human spirit. Stories focus on characters — what they do, and what happens to them. Stories can be very effective ways for healthcare providers and educators to address real life issues.

Austin, N. (September 1996). Working Woman, 14-18.

Langer, N. (2009). Using narratives in healthcare communication. Educational Gerontology, 35; 55-62, 2009.

On My Way Out

Reviewed by Erris Langer Klapper
Pittsburgh, PA

While dating and contemplating the formula for finding the right life partner, documentarian Brandon Gross relied on two life-long experts, turning the camera on his beloved grandparents. After all, what better source for hands-on advice on the subject of everlasting love and commitment than his grandparents, who had been married for 65 years? Along with his co-director Skyler Gross, Brandon set out to interview his grandparents and, in the process, inadvertently put a spotlight on what would become his family's greatest revelation: That his cherished Nani and Popi kept a secret their entire lives together and that their relationship was far more complicated than anyone realized.

"On My Way Out: The Secret Life of Nani And Popi" is a must- see film in which Popi reveals that he is gay.

Nani and Popi were born in Europe, met before the war and reunited in the aftermath of surviving the horrors of the Holocaust. They married, immigrated to Los Angeles and had two daughters. To the outside world, Nani and Popi embodied the American Dream. Popi always knew he was gay and says he was born into a world that didn't understand human nature. Nani found out by mistake when she called a bathhouse he was supposedly visiting but was told he hadn't been there that day. When she confronted him, he told her the truth. Their decision to hide the secret and continue their life together stemmed from their staunch and cherished belief that marriage is for life. No wonder their grandson looked towards them for their secret, and in doing so, uncovered a far deeper one.

As altruistic as the "married for life" sentiment may sound, there is an underlying theme of lack of choice, which Popi articulates to his grandson, stating that his options were to either commit suicide or live in a closet. "I decided to live," he says. This is a sentiment often echoed by Holocaust survivors, and the irony of surviving a concentration camp and still not living freely is not lost on the audience.

The pure magic of this film is the portrayal of a deep and beautiful relationship that is perhaps flawed, but real and devoted. Nani gave Popi the space to be himself within the confines of societal pressures at the time, and he remained committed to their closely-knit family. There is nothing phony in finding out that this marriage is not what it seemed; in fact, there is something even more compelling in discovering that their commitment to each other was life-long despite a difficult and complicated reality.

Never talking about their secret was part of the deal that Nani and Popi made, but secrets weigh heavily and take their toll. At 95, Popi feels the need to unburden himself and live an authentic life to its fullest. "For 90 years I was in pain and still am. Why should I take it to my grave?" Popi is open and forthcoming on his way out of both the closet and the material world and has come to terms with his sexuality, humanity and true self. Nani remains closed, having kept the I secret she was hoping she'd take to her grave. Nani has dementia, which is perhaps a saving grace for her as the audience senses that she would never have agreed to discuss the secret otherwise. In one scene, she denies admitting to her daughter that Popi is gay.

Although the revelation rocks and upends everything the family knew as true and real, the acceptance and support they provide to Nani and Popi are unconditional and profound. While Popi may not have been lucky enough to be born into a generation that is accepting of his sexuality and identity, he experiences the openness and recognition across generations within his own family, allowing him to exit this world with honesty and dignity.

This film provides an intimate and powerful birds-eye view into the most private of marriages, without a shred of voyeuristic or prurient intent. Empathetically breaking stereotypes, the film makes us realize that we all have secrets and Popi's need to unburden himself is instinctive and life affirming. Grandchildren often look at their grandparents as heroes who spoil, adore and admire them unconditionally

without any of the rules and judgments inherent in parenting. Brandon's pursuit of his grandparents' secret to a successful marriage and life partnership stems from his admiration of their commitment and longevity. Admirably, when he inadvertently uncovers an utterly unexpected secret, he and his family do not stand in judgment, wringing their hands and declaring that it was all a lie. Instead, they rally to support both Nani and Popi with grace. "On My Way Out: The Secret Life of Nani and Popi," is a short but extremely powerful lesson in unconditional love, generational support, acceptance and empathy.

"WHO MOVED MY CHEESE?"
ADJUSTING TO AGE-RELATED CHANGES

By Nieli Langer
Educational Gerontology
38 (7)459-464; 2012

The book, "Who Moved My Cheese?" (Johnson, 1998) is a metaphor for change. This parable-like story mirrors the life-altering changes that face aging individuals. The four characters in the book are looking for their "Cheese" in a maze. Cheese represents whatever makes people happy. How each character adjusts to the loss of Cheese parallels the process of adjusting to one or more of the many transitions in the lives of older adults. The character Hem fears change so he resists and denies it while Haw learns to adapt when he is confronted with change. Sniff senses change early while Scurry gets right down to action in the light of impending changes. The straightforward lesson of "moving with the cheese" may help adults understand and cope with changes as they age and propel health care and social service professionals toward a workable approach to change with their clients that provides positive opportunities for effective adaptation.

Aging brings many types of changes. It is a challenging period in people's lives that often includes sudden and multiple losses and unforeseen physical, emotional, social, economic and spiritual assaults to their person. Despite adversity, older people adjust successfully, continue to embrace life with enthusiasm, and face new challenges with strength and determination (e.g., the character, Haw). Others, in like circumstances, are crushed by the weight of their lives, vulnerable and helpless, and withdraw into themselves (the character, Hem). The extent to which they accept and adapt to changes directly affects the quality of life they can achieve and maintain as they grow older.

Adaptation is the process of adjusting to fit a situation or environment. Changes that require adaptation can occur either within the individual and/or in his/her situation or environment. These changes may be automatic and require minimal effort (the characters Sniff and Scurry instinctively address their altered situation) or demand non-routine responses to alleviate the stress that accompanies the change (the character, Haw). People may adapt to age changes in appearance gradually and routinely, whereas adapting to sudden and severe disability usually requires all the coping skills and social support they can muster. To adjust to a change, a person needs to acknowledge that a change has occurred. Failure to acknowledge the change delays adaptation and an internal reconciliation with an external reality (Ruth & Coleman, 1996). In the story *"Who Moved My Cheese?"* changes are described as unavoidable and holding promise rather than as a stumbling block or dead end.

The way in which a person perceives the significance of an adverse event to his well-being is referred to as *cognitive appraisal*, first described by Lazarus and Delongis (1983). Cognitive appraisal means that different people can view the same situation differently. This assessment serves to minimize or magnify the scale or stressfulness of an event by attaching some significance to it. Coping is the manner in which a person responds to stress: the cognitive, emotional, and behavioral responses made in the face of internally and externally created events. Coping responses may include *instrumental*, i.e., taking action to ease the stress; *intrapsychic*, i.e., acceptance of the situation; *affective*, i.e., expressing strong emotions about the stressor; *escape*, i.e. avoiding or denying the problem; and, *resigned helplessness*, i.e., unable to cope (Kahana & Kahana, 1982). If an event is judged to be benign, it may elicit minimal coping responses. However, if the situation is construed as harmful or threatening, the individual's adaptation responses are alerted (Lazarus & Delongis, 1983; Folkman, Lazarus. & Novacek, 1987). One individual may see it as a challenge (positive stressor; Haw character), while another will view it as a threat (negative stressor; Hem character).

Continuity is an important adaptive strategy used by many people as they age (Atchley, 2000). Continuity does not negate change; it does, however, signify that new life experiences have occurred against a known and constant solid background for both the individual and his/her environment. The two mice, Sniff and Scurry noticed that the Cheese supply in the maze was diminishing. They did not overanalyze; they untied their running shoes and ventured into the maze in pursuit of the tried-and-true activity of their existence, i.e., finding the Cheese. When a life-alerting situation occurred and the Cheese had moved, they changed and moved with the Cheese. Continuity was instinctual to their existence. Many older people rely on continuity in their lives because it appears necessary for their security and survival. Continuity of activities and environments concentrates the individual's energies in familiar domains of activity where learned routines can minimize the effects of aging.

How an older person attempts to alleviate the stresses that accompany age-related changes influences his/her long-term well-being. Self-esteem is a person's emotional assessment about his/her identity relative to the ability to adjust to the stressors of aging. An individual who experiences multiple role losses must not only adapt to the lifestyle changes associated with aging such as financial insecurity or a shrinking social network, but also integrate the new roles into his/her best self or learn to amend what best is. Older persons, experiencing multiple physical and cognitive disabilities concurrently with role losses, must cope with multiple challenges at a time in their lives when they have the fewest resources to resolve them successfully (Hooyman & Kiyak, 2005).

The idea of successful aging should never be based on denial of real losses of function as people age. Psychologists are interested in understanding why some individuals adapt more easily to the challenges of aging than others. Therefore, they attach special meaning to the term "successful aging." The term does not suggest optimal or problem-free; it implies that individuals are satisfied or content with their lives — that they have found ways of maximizing the positive in their lives while minimizing the impact of inevitable age-related losses (Baltes & Carstensen, 1996). "We cannot predict what any given individual's successful aging will look like until we know what are the domains of functioning and goals that that individual considers important, personally meaningful and in which he/she feels competent." (Baltes & Carstensen, 1996, p. 399). Psychologists as well as gerontologists, therefore, focus on the meaning and well-being that individuals preserve in the face of objective losses in mind, body and environment (Vaillant, 2002).

Selective optimization with compensation (Baltes & Baltes, 1990; Grove, Loeb & Penrod, 2009) is a practical definition of successful aging. With age, available resources (cognitive, physical, social, and economic) may begin to shrink; as a result, the selection pressure on individuals becomes even greater. As people age, it becomes harder to balance multiple roles and sustain multiple activities. As a result, many people reduce the number of domains in which they are active. The idea of selective optimization refers to an individual's decision to gradually narrow the range of the capabilities he/she seeks to maintain to those which are most functional to his/her current life stage. If older adults conserve their resources for the domains that are most significant to them, the authors contend, older adults may be able to maintain adaptive functioning for longer periods. The second process, *compensation*, refers to people's ability to seek new ways of accomplishing things that become difficult or impossible because of losses in functional capacity (Baltes & Baltes, 1990). To the extent that older individuals are successful in compensating for change and eventual losses, they may be able to prolong their period of active life involvement. The measure of successful aging, then, is life satisfaction and a sense of well-being in the face of decline (Gignac, Cott, & Badley, 2002).

Hem and Haw arrived at the cheese station, and having taken their cheese for granted, were surprised to find there was no more cheese. They felt the situation was unfair. They remained in cheese station with the expectation that the cheese would return one day. It never did. As time passed, they were getting weaker and more tired; age, too, was no longer on their side. Haw realized that they needed to do things differently. Realizing that change is the only thing that is constant in life, he moved into the maze looking for *New Cheese* in different places, taking alternative routes until he found it. Doing the same things over and over again and wondering why things don't get better is unproductive. He realized it was natural for change to continually occur, whether you expect it or not. He began to understand that when you change what you believe, you change what you do. He decided to adapt to the change rather than simply letting things happen to him. Movement in a new direction helped him to stop being fearful and to finally find *New Cheese.*

Hem, on the other hand, railed against his bad fortune; change wasn't right or fair. He had been comfortable in his own sense of self and in his situation; he was fearful of change and paralyzed to do anything about it. "I don't think I would like New Cheese. It's not what I'm used to. I want my own cheese back and I'm not going to change until I get what I want." (Johnson, 1998, p.61). Fear that a person allows to build up in his/her mind is often worse than the situational reality. Some people confront and resolve the changes that aging poses while others refuse to adapt. Some have never learned to cope well with change and have retreated in the face of change throughout their lives. They do not know how to evaluate or what to expect from change; nor have they had the experience of setting realistic goals for adaptation. People who repeatedly experience failure to adapt often develop feelings of hopelessness and engage in a variety of self-harming behaviors.

For older adults, changes that ultimately result in deprivations often translate into fewer opportunities: shrinking an individual's feelings of competence and self-worth; physical frailty; and, loss of independence. If older persons perceive that the changes in their lives rob them of their identity and, therefore, their independence, often begin to feel valueless or useless. When losses make older adults feel frightened, uncertain of a future direction or threaten their independence, they feel more vulnerable and less in control of their lives. The extent to which they accept and adapt to these losses with or without professional guidance and family support directly affects the quality of life they can continue to maintain.

Unfortunately, all too often, older adults, assaulted by multiple losses, simply give up areas of activity that they once enjoyed and become depressed by the cumulative changes with which they are confronted. One way of protecting against the negative consequences of giving up is to *reconceptualize* what is important. It is this process that researchers have termed *flexible goal adjustment* (Brandtstadter, Wentura, & Greve, 1993) or secondary control (Heckhausen & Schultz, 1995). Both concepts suggest that as people age, they become increasingly likely to relinquish some goals and willing to modify and reduce their expectations. Aging adults play a selective role in choosing to adopt and elaborate past and possible selves that are consistent with or support desired self-esteem, and to discard or modify those that are incompatible. In this way, they still remain firmly in charge of managing the adaptive processes by which they can maintain high levels of well-being and meaning- making in their lives (Markus & Hertzog, 1991). People cannot always change their destinies, but they are often able to change their directions.

Vaillant (2002) observed that those who had aged well in light of some adversity shared the quality of *resilience*, i.e., the ability to restore balance following a difficult experience and integrate it into the backdrop of total life experiences. For example, retired individuals may explore new roles by participating in volunteer activities or being active mentors or grandparents. Some older adults are able to cope with declining health, making adjustments as needed. Wagnild & Young (1990) identified themes that provide the foundation for resiliency. Perseverance refers to persistence in the face of adversity or discouragement. Many older people refer to a survival instinct or a drive to keep going which equates with perseverance. *Self-reliance* is a belief in oneself and one's inherent capabilities. Very often self- reliance emerges after older adults are challenged (e.g., some loss of physical functioning) to find resources within themselves to manage and maintain daily activities. Having successfully resolved the challenge, they feel more self-sufficient and confident to resume their lives.

An important aspect of adjustment to aging and loss is the ability to derive meaning from experiences and the realization that life has a purpose, *meaningfulness* (Wagnild & Young, 1990). When people are capable of transforming negative events into opportunities, the result is personal growth and life satisfaction (Langer, 2004). Personal meaning is a collection of themes of life's domains that have been, and will continue to be essential to a person's existence. These themes provide an individual with purpose as well as an identity. The meaning and purpose derived from life themes define spirituality. If a person is conscious of his/her own life themes (i.e. family, individual growth, creativity, religion, legacy) spirituality is played out through the ordinary and the everyday events of his/her life and existence is charged with meaning (Fiske & Chiriboga, 1991; Hedlund & Birren, 1984; Thurner, 1975).

Spirituality becomes a "personal compass" by which an individual can assess and navigate his/her current needs. An older adult may experience many losses and yet retain a general sense of well-being and the conviction that life has meaning. Baltes and Baltes (1990) noted that even with pronounced signs of frailty, aging adults are capable of making necessary modifications in goals and aspirations. When an individual continues to develop through his life experiences and finds sources of meaning (spirituality) therein, he/she is more empowered to cope with life's stresses and survive.

While many older persons lead fulfilling lives, others feel a loss of meaning and purpose (the character, Hem). Whereas some older adults find ways to adapt to the vicissitudes of getting old, many may require the assistance of professionals to help reclaim or reaffirm their identity or spirituality. The professional can often help clients view how they may use their spirituality as an effective coping strategy for life's losses and stressors, as a source for reframing crises, and as a source of strength for facing the future. When the professional caregiver is seen to value the client's spirituality, the client is empowered to use the coping mechanisms he/she already has in place. With appropriate opportunity to articulate their life themes and issues, these troubled older adults may be counseled into resolving some of their difficulties.

Social service and health care providers have witnessed and participated in the care of individuals who they believed to possess the quality of inner strength when faced with adversity or loss. Assessing clients' spirituality and resiliency in its various expressions, identifying its use, and including it in individual counseling interventions may assist older clients to recognize their capacity to readjust during periods of disruption and loss. They are empowered to utilize the strengths they already possess (Langer 2000; Gray 2005).

Identifying strengths in the clients' environment minimizes the possibility of clients being blamed for their circumstances. The *strengths perspective* focuses on capabilities, assets, and positive attributes rather than problems and pathologies. All subsequent phases of professional intervention hinge on the type and qualitative attributes of the assessment. Saleebey (1992) has captured the rationale of the strength's perspective assessment with the following challenge:

> At the very least, the strengths perspective obligates counselors to understand that however downtrodden or sick, individuals have survived (and in some cases even thrived). They have taken steps, summoned up resources and coped. We need to know what they have done, how they have done it, what they have learned from doing it, and which resources (inner and outer) were available in their struggle to surmount their troubles. People are always working on their situations, even if just deciding to be resigned to them; as helpers we must tap into that work, elucidate it, and find and build on its possibilities (pp. 171-2).

As social service providers gather information in their assessment of clients, they discover that these individuals do not conform to stereotypes; they hear stories of survival and resiliency where clients withstood encroaching changes and losses and rerouted their life goals (Friedrich, 2001).

The four imaginary characters, Sniff, Scurry, Hem and Haw represent both the simple and complex parts of each human being. Sometimes we sniff out change and scurry into action. At other times we deny and resist change while at other times we learn to adapt on our own or with family and professional support and realize that the change and adaptation has produced something better. Changes will indeed occur; those who come to terms with them alone, or with the support of the informal and/or formal social networks, will have the potential to maximize the quality of their lives.

The Ties of Later Life: Aging Siblings

Jillmosleylanger@gmail.com
Mathew Love mlovel9@utk.edu; University of Tennessee

Abstract

The study sought to investigate whether aging siblings (ages 60-91) have expectations of social support from their brothers and sisters. Social support includes emotional (expressive) and tangible (instrumental) assistance. One hundred, noninstitutionalized older adults with at least one older sibling volunteered to respond to the survey. The respondents were drawn from several YMCAs in Knoxville, Tennessee, that sponsor Silver Sneakers, a senior athletic program. Factors mediating family solidarity included frequency of association, quality of affection, degree of exchange of services, and level of filial obligations. These variables provided the context for the development of an instrument for the determination of older sibling ties. Contrary to the hypothesis that female siblings would share affectual solidarity, the opposite was true. The study revealed that older female siblings rarely expect and receive expressive support from one another. Neither expects nor receives instrumental support, mostly attributed to distance. However, regardless of the lack of either expressive or instrumental support, older siblings responded that they thought the relationship was very important (74%); they felt close to their female sibling (53%); and, 60% wanted the same level of contact while 39% sought even greater contact. The behavioral reality of older sibling relations suggests that family ties, regardless of actual contact or provision of helping activities, remains strong.

Introduction

Sibling relationships are the longest relationship that most individuals share — a quality that makes sibling relationships unique but that is universal regardless of nationality or geographic location. Qualities such as contact, help and support, feelings of closeness and security are markers of sibling attachment into adulthood and those behaviors, in turn, are related to linked psychological and physical health in old age (Cicirelli, 1995). One universal common denominator is that people change over time and as they do, their relationships and interactions with siblings may evolve, too.

Research on older sibling relationships lags behind other family relationships. In addition, no single theoretical psychologically oriented perspective can inform research on older sibling relationships. (Whiteman, McHale & Soli, 2011). An accumulating body of work, however, documents that sibling relations are central in the lives of individuals and families around the world and across the life span (Connidis & Campbell, 1995).

Sibling relationships are unique in that they are characterized by both hierarchical and reciprocal elements, which change across place and time. Some older siblings get stuck in childhood roles such as the surrogate parent or protector of younger siblings. Research has described at least 5 types of adult sibling relationships: (1) Intimate — extremely devoted; (2) Congenial — close and caring friends but marriage partner and parent/child relationships exceed sibling relations; (3) Loyal — based on common family history and obligation; (4) Apathetic — lack of connectedness; (5) Hostile — resentful and angry (Tiret, 2014).

The findings of a qualitative examination of sibling relationships in old age revealed that interactions with sisters and brothers took on new meaning in late life. A shared history of lifetime experiences made the sibling relationship unique in social networks in old age. Those who had positive relationships with siblings found that interactions decreased feelings of loneliness, provided emotional support and validation of earlier life expectations, and built feelings of closeness and sibling solidarity. Even those who had negative sibling relationships indicated a shift in feelings. The intensity of feeling about siblings in old age suggests that further study of the later-life sibling bond might increase understanding of ways in which the social and emotional needs of older people can be met (Gold, 1987).

Research suggests that older people perceive the informal social network of kin as the most appropriate source of social support in most situations. Family members are seen by older people as natural extensions of themselves (Suitor, Gillegan & Pillener, 2019; Gullen, Mills, & Jump (2003). Emphasis on the family arises from both the family's centrality in providing social care and its primacy in the lives of the elderly. Basic to the concept of a social support system is the idea that the assistance provided is a means of augmenting individual competency and mastery over the environment rather than increasing dependency. However, there is paucity of information on the patterns of aging sibling exchange of support, affective or tangible.

One major asset of supportive sibling relationships is that it can theoretically function as a resource for the individuals and families as a whole by helping to absorb family pressures and provide assistance. Practically, the sibling dyad is a potential resource for the elderly in providing a wider circle of nurturance and support. Human service practitioners need to strengthen this link by awareness of the level of expressive (emotional support) and tangible (instrumental) exchange of assistance that exists between aging siblings.

Assistance within the family tends to be based on a system of mutual reciprocity stretching over the life cycle. However, the presence of a support element alone is insufficient to assure meaningful assistance. In order for a support element to be considered "functional," there must be evidence of an ongoing relationship to guarantee meaningful support between the dyad (Antonucci (1985); Suitor, Gillegan, & Pillener, 2019). Functional solidarity is a construct that measures the exchange of assistance and support between and within generations. The frequency of exchange of services as well as the perception of potential support between generations or within the generational dyad are measures of functional solidarity.

Socialization within the family is a process of ongoing bilateral negotiation. In the case of sibling relations, in order for this negotiation to proceed, each sibling must recognize the needs and motivations of their siblings. Therefore, a sibling's expectations of service from his/her sibling will reflect the previous history of the kin relationship between them and the current needs and concerns of each. The supports provided can be of an instrumental nature involving direct tangible assistance, or of an affective nature involving solely emotional support. The opportunity to both give and receive support from a sibling is critical to an individual's assessment of and satisfaction with his/her social network.

Method

A 25-item questionnaire measured both the objective and subjective aspects of kinship relations between aging siblings with whom the respondent perceived to have the closest relationship. Interactional characteristics included size of family network, frequency and kinds of association (affective support), and services exchanged (tangible services).

Sample

The target for the study was the population of noninstitutionalized older siblings with at least one brother or sister with whom they felt a bond. The sample consisted of 100 senior citizens (ages 60-91) who frequented the YMCA of Greater Knoxville (Tennessee, USA) as participants in the Silver Sneakers sports program. They constitute a middle-class population of senior citizens who drive themselves to these venues. The average respondent was female, married, in self-declared good health whose closest sibling (usually a sister) lived out of state.

Results

Seventy-four percent of respondents consider the sibling relationship to be very important and 53% describe the relationship as very close. While 60% want the same level of contact, 39% sought greater contact. Even though the majority of respondents did not share either affectual or tangible support, 68% responded that they would want to be 6 declared good health whose closest sibling (usually a sister) more supportive of their sibling.

Discussion

The healthiest adult sibling relationships are either congenial or loyal. Viewing older siblings as close friends coupled with family loyalty can become supportive as one grows older and the social circle upon which one previously depended upon diminishes. Many of the respondents view sibling relationships as an hour glass effect, i.e., very close growing up, slim to no interaction in the teen and young adult years, then seeking to greater contact as they aged.

Sibling functioning generally involves feelings of satisfaction that one member gains from doing things for or caring for the other. This includes not only concrete instrumental assistance, but also emotional support. Exchange reflects the assistance provided and received by both siblings.

The results of the measure on sibling expectations of support revealed that sibling respondents had negligible expectations of meaningful expressive support, i.e. visiting, telephone contact while having even lower expectations of instrumental support, i.e., shopping and/or driving, etc.

The homogeneity of the study sample in terms of health and socio-economic levels restricts the generalizability of the findings. This lack of generalizability is not necessarily a problem; the goal of the study was not to test causal relationships which requires representative samples, but to generate hypotheses on the service expectations of aging siblings. The findings provide insight into an under-researched category of the elderly. These findings should be viewed as hypotheses that await systematic testing on a representative sample.

Conclusion

Assistance within the family has consistently been based on a system of mutual reciprocity stretching over the life cycle. The role of informal supports in providing affective support is crucial and can be as important as the provision of instrumental support. Implications for social-work/gerontology policy practice suggests that siblings are an integral part of the informal support system.

Improvements in life expectancy have changed the structure of multigenerational families; joint survivorship within and across generations has resulted in extended periods of support exchanges (including caregiving) and affective connections over the life span. At the same time, relationships in aging families have become more fluid and less predictable, as reduced fertility and increased rates of divorce, remarriage, and stepfamily formation have altered an the micro context in which intergenerational, spousal, and sibling relations function. The implications of increased diversity in kinship structures for such practical outcomes as support and caregiving to older family members have yet to be parsed but remain important concerns in light of declining filial commitment and the aging of support providers and recipients.

Research on aging families has only begun to use person- centered approaches that treat individuals as embedded within a web of family affiliations and responsibilities. For example, middle-aged persons often occupy several family roles simultaneously (e.g., spouse, sibling, child of an older parent, parent to an adult child, grandparent to a young grandchild); therefore, it is important to examine these role demands in combination when assessing their impact on individual well-being and the ability of family members to include future care for aging siblings.

The study of aging families calls for a greater focus on how practical assistance, resource sharing, and kinship obligations have been affected by the emergence of new family forms caused by declines in fertility, and increases in divorce, remarriage, non-marital childbearing, and grandparent-headed households. We need to consider an integrated life-course approach that considers multiple family actors over the entire life span.

An ambitious agenda lies ahead, one that requires data that do not yet exist and methodologies still to be perfected. We need expanded use of longitudinal data. We will continue to investigate if later life is adequately being served by family networks. We can probably be optimistic, given historical evidence showing time and again the resilience of family life to altered environmental conditions.

References

Antonucci, T. (1985). Reciprocal and nonreciprocal social support: in *Handbook of aging and the social sciences* (2nd edition). R. Binstock and E. Shanas (eds.) Van Nostrand Reinhold: New York.

Cicirelli V. (1995). *Sibling relationships across the life span.* New York: Plenum Press.

Connidis I., Campbell L. (1995). Closeness, confiding, and contact among siblings in middle adulthood. *J Family Issues.* 16:722-745.

Gillen, M., Mills T., & Jump, J. (2003). *Family Relationships in an Aging Society.* University of Florida. First published: May 2003. Revised: November 2012.

Gold, D. (1987). Siblings in old age: something special. *Canadian J on Aging.* 6(3):199-216.

Port, C., Zimmerman, L., Christianna S., et al. (2005). Families Filling the Gap: Comparing Family Involvement for Assisted Living and Nursing in *The Gerontologist.* The Gerontological Society of America. Vol 45, Special Issue I, 2005.

Sousa, Liliana (eds.) (2009). *Families in later life: Emerging themes and challenges.* Nova Science Publishers: New York

Suitor, J., Gillegan, M., Pillener, K (2019). *Handbook of aging and the social sciences* (8th edition). Ferraro, K, & George, L (eds.); Academic Press: San Diego, California.

Tiret, H (2014). The importance of adult sibling relationships. Michigan State University Extension.

Whiteman, S., McHale S., Soli A. (2011). Theoretical perspectives on sibling relationships. *J Fam Theory Review* 3(2): 124-139.

What Makes an In-law an Outlaw?

Mm . . . let me count the ways . . .

This infomercial is dedicated to my new in-law, Beverley. When God created her, He threw away the mold. He also embraced me for all the years of having the patience of Job in my relationships with the now discarded (through divorce and/or disgust) of 3 sets of outlaws.

My now banished in-laws have a roomful of higher degrees but are clueless in emotional intelligence. If a person is aware of his/her emotional responses as they occur, they can begin to regulate how they influence their actions. However, either through stupidity or arrogance, my outlaws sucked the air out of any room they entered. I don't always accept the adage . . . ''you cain't fix stupid,' because you can often teach people if you have patience and skill. However, you 'cain't fix arrogance.

Arrogant people have such high opinions of themselves, that they believe that only their knowledge and experience are worth adhering to. It's okay to cut toxic family members out of your life. Blood ain't thicker than peace of mind. Adam and Eve were the happiest and luckiest people in the world because neither of them had mothers-in-law.

Some Banned and Challenged Books: 2010-2023

In light of the current societal crisis, that has affected every component of our lives, I have decided to share the following banned book list. I would never advise what/what not to read but it behooves us to be aware of the current literary and educational crisis we are facing. 1, for one, will begin to purchase these books for my grandchildren so they will not be deprived of what I think is the world's valuable stories.

The Absolutely True Diary of a Part-Time Indian by Sherman Alexie

Captain Underpants (series) by Dav Pilkey

Looking for Alaska by John Green

George by Alex Gino

And Tango Makes Three by Justin Richardson and Peter Parnell

Drama by Raina Telgemeier

Fifty Shades of Grey by E. L. James

The Bluest Eye by Toni Morrison

The Kite Runner by Khaled Hosseini

Hunger Games by Suzanne Collins

I Am Jazz by Jazz Jennings and Jessica Herthel

The Perks of Being a Wallflower by Stephen Chbosky

To Kill a Mockingbird by Harper Lee

Bone (series) by Jeff Smith

The Glass Castle by Jeannette Walls

Two Boys Kissing by David Levithan

A Day in the Life of Marlon Bundo by Jill Twiss

Sex is a Funny Word by Cory Silverberg

Alice McKinley (series) by Phyllis Reynolds Naylor

It's Perfectly Normal by Robie H. Harris

Nineteen Minutes by Jodi Picoult

Scary Stories (series) by Alvin Schwartz

Speak by Laurie Halse Anderson

A Brave New World by Aldous Huxley

Of Mice and Men by John Steinbeck

The Handmaid's Tale by Margaret Atwood

The Hate U Give by Angie Thomas

Fun Home: A Family Tragicomic by Alison Bechdel

It's a Book by Lane Smith

The Adventures of Huckleberry Finn by Mark Twain

The Things They Carried by Tim O'Brien

My Mother Doesn't Know by Sonya What Sones

A Child Called "It" by Dave Pelzer

Bad Kitty (series) by Nick Bruel

Crank by Ellen Hopkins

Nickel and dimed by Barbara Ehrenreich

Persepolis by Marjane Satrapi

The Adventures of Super Diaper Baby by Dav Pilkey

This Day in June by Gayle E. Pitman

This One Summer by Mariko Tamaki

A Bad Boy Can Be Good for A Girl by Tanya Lee Stone

Beloved by Toni Morrison

Extremely Loud & Incredibly Close by Jonathan Safran Foer

Gossip Girl (series) by Cecily von Ziegesar.

House of Night (series) by P.C. Cast

1984 by George Orwell

Almost Perfect by Brian Katcher

Awakening by Kate Chopin

Burned by Ellen Hopkins

Ender's Game by Orson Scott Card

Fallen Angels by Walter Dean Myers

Glass by Ellen Hopkins

Heather Has Two Mommies by Newman

I Know Why the Caged Bird Sings by Maya Angelou

Madeline and the Gypsies by Ludwig Bemelmans

My Princess Boy by Cheryl Kyodais

Prince and Knight by Daniel Haack

Revolutionary Voices: A Multicultural Queer Youth Anthology by Amy Sonnie

Skippyjon Jones (series) by Judith Schachner

So far from the Bamboo Grove by Yoko Kawashima Watkins

The Color of Earth (series) by Tong-hwa Kim

The Librarian of Basra by Jeanette Winter

The Walking Dead (series) by Robert Kirkman

Tricks by Ellen Hopkins

Uncle Bobby's Wedding by Sarah S Brannen

To the McMinn County Schools, Tennessee

Why the schools need to reconsider allowing students to read the graphic novel, MAUS by Art Spiegelman.

Over the years, many books have been removed by school boards and libraries. When a book is removed and /or banned, it deprives people of the opportunity to learn the facts about history, the world, and the truth. My grandfather was a researcher and physician who frequently lectured all over the world. His first sentence at every lecture began with these words: "You are all entitled to your opinions, but you <u>are not</u> entitled to your own facts." By removing Maus, the school board is denying students the opportunity to learn the facts about the Holocaust in a very unique way. If a picture is worth a thousand words, then Maus, with cats as Nazi guards and mice as their victims, helps readers, in this original art form, to get closer to the experience of the Holocaust. The book, through words and pictures gives the reader the opportunity to look into the hearts of two survivors, Art and his father, Vladek, and make their experience the reader's experience.

At the Holocaust Museum in Washington, young visitors are given the biography of a young victim and they move through the Museum as if they were this person. The experience makes it real for each young visitor. The author, Pat Conroy, once wrote about the Holocaust, "one English word should not be required to carry so many human hearts" (Conroy, 1995) Beach Music. Bantam books: New York, p. 628.)

We students need to learn not only facts and history but also about people who have overcome major obstacles to be called "heroes." Vladek, Spiegelman's father, was a hero and survivor. It must have taken heroic stamina and luck for a Jew to make it out of Auschwitz alive. Vladek uses every opportunity available to save himself and his wife.

We need to imagine ourselves in comparable situations in order to understand what pushed Vladek to do what he did. Some of us need to learn how to model courageous behavior.

Granddaughter's English assignment . . .

Who Did You Used to Be?

Having celebrated my 77th birthday, I was asked by a thirty-something person, *"Who did you used to be?"*

Did the question imply that my age disqualified me as currently being relevant or useful and that only my younger self fulfilled a valuable place in society?

Age is frequently overworked and misused. Irrational prejudice often occurs in judging a person's capabilities on the basis of the characteristics of a conditioned age group and what we presume as being appropriate and typical of that age set. We cannot anticipate the changes that will be brought about by population aging by looking back in history because the current concepts are unprecedented in human history. The rules of aging have been forever altered as the lifestyles and life cycles of the current older population are continually being reinvented.

The members of the Davis Y (Knoxville, TN) water aerobics club comprises an eclectic and exclusive group of accomplished individuals who, throughout their lives, have influenced their respective communities. They represent an honor roll of nonprofessional and professional expertise that swims with us 6 days/week and continues to positively affect our individual and combined communities. Our special class would not succeed without recognizing the efforts of first class instructors coupled with an energetic Y staff of professionals.

Most of us realize that we have 2 assets that we can use to make the world a little better place...**time and wisdom.** While they might be the most obvious resources that a senior has, time is rarely used constructively. Using our now open schedules to assist in our communities can bring more personal satisfaction than simply staying home. The medical value of keeping our minds and bodies alert and active has positive value, too.

In Number Our Days (1978), the late anthropologist Barbara Meyerhof borrowed from the Psalmists who urged..."teach us to number our days that we may get a heart of wisdom." (Pirke Avot; ethics of the Fathers of Judaism). What is a heart of wisdom? This question provides us with the possibility of making choices. Each stage of our life provides its own lessons and joys. Some of us may come to learn that our strengths lie not in the activities of our youth but in those of our own personal power to effect positive change as we age.

In Pirke Avot, Hillel, a Jewish sage, continued by asking: "if I am for myself alone, what am I?" If we are solely for ourselves, we overlook and neglect the needs and aspirations of others. Most of us will continue to teach, heal, mentor in our communities and in our families. Finally, HIllel asks "...and if not now, when?" Getting older means that there isn't always time; will we bother with stuff that does not mean much to us? In interpreting the last of HIllel's questions, we are reminded that we may not always get the same opportunity again.

If nature has prolonged our lives 25-40 years, it is important to create/discover our purpose in the bigger picture and to use our living and evolving wisdom for the good of ourselves and others.. Rabbi Tarfon, a second century scholar reminds us: "You are not required to complete the work, but neither are you free to desist from it..." (Pirke Avot).

Life is About Finding People
Who Are Your Kind of Crazy . . .

Did you ever notice that as we get older and our eyesight dims, our ability to see through bullshit becomes more powerful?!?

Foreign Ports . . .

I haven't mentioned all our foreign travels due to my husband's professional obligations. We have been to Paris, London, Poland, Greece, Cyprus, Turkey, Hungary, the Czech Republic, Germany, Italy, Mexico, Norway, Sweden, Holland, Israel, Panama, Argentine, Australia, Sardinia, New Zealand, Austria, Switzerland, India and China.

The South African adventure, in the height of Apartheid, left a lasting impression on our family. My husband and I once mistakenly waited at a Blacks Only bus stop and only belatedly realized why the driver wasn't stopping! Registered as foreign nationals, almost every incoming phone call to our home was monitored, even those in which we spoke Hebrew. We regularly heard the telltale click as the control switch was turned on.

We were living in a fascist regime in which you could be detained by the authorities for failure to pay a parking ticket in a timely fashion! A close friend once badgered me to immediately write a check and mail it for a parking infraction because he, as a South African, knew what the repercussions could be.

A very disturbing event occurred when my mother- in-law visited us in Johannesburg. Anna, our live-in housekeeper, wanted to surprise her by baking a cake in her honor. I gave Anna sufficient funds to cover the cost of the ingredients and she walked the short block to the shop. Once there, she was accosted by two young white males who demanded to know where she had gotten the money. They smacked her around and chased a bleeding Anna back to our house. Bruised and limping, she told us her story. Meanwhile, the men began to threaten us with retribution for defending Anna. We were all so traumatized by this event that we still talk about it almost 40 year later!

The Bantustans or homelands, established by the Apartheid Government in the mid-1950s, were underdeveloped areas to which the majority of the Black population was moved in order to prevent them from living in the White urban areas of South Africa. This administrative mechanism separated Blacks from Whites and gave Blacks the responsibility of running their own independent governments. However, it denied them the protection and any remaining rights a Black could have in South Africa. In other words, homelands were established for the permanent removal of the Black population from White South Africa.

For example, if a Black man or woman was of Zulu origin, they were assigned to KwaZulu, the homeland designed for Zulus. Ten homelands, designed for specific ethnic groups were created in South Africa such as Transkei, Bophuthatswana, Ciskei, etc. Millions of Blacks had to leave their homelands daily and work in the mines, for White farmers, or as domestics including other industries in the cities in order to make a living. The homelands served as labor reservoirs, housing the unemployed and releasing them when their labor was needed in White South Africa.

Pass laws became one of the dominant features of the country's Apartheid system. The Black populace was required to carry these passes (identification cards) with them when outside their homelands. Failure to produce a pass often resulted in imprisonment.

When we left South Africa, we could only dream that racial and social equality would be achieved without a bloodbath. Two very powerful movies that depict the before/after history of South Africa: A Dry White Season (also a book) by Andre Brink (during Apartheid) & Invictus (Black President Mandel's arranged rugby match to encourage racial interaction).

Schmaltz Anyone?

Schmaltz is rendered chicken or goose fat used in cooking or as a spread. It was once considered essential to Ashkenazi Jewish cooking in Europe. When you are a visiting Jewish professor in Poland in the '90s, what subjects were safe to discuss without being politically incorrect?!?

1. The number of professionals who whispered in your ear that they were Jewish and that they hid their religious heritage from blatant anti-Semitism in Polish academia?
2. The beautiful synagogue you wanted to visit but was advised it had since been renovated into the municipal swimming pool?

In an effort to find common ground, food is always a neutral yet energizing topic to share. The Department Chair and the visiting professor, both with Polish backgrounds, found common ground exchanging the "culinary" qualities of schmaltz. At the airport, the Chair bid farewell to her guest and as a parting gift, ceremoniously presented him with a jar of schmaltz. He thanked her profusely. In the departure lounge, he hid the bottle of schmaltz behind a chair. With the announcement to board and now free of the schmaltz, the professor walked to the plane. An airport attendant spotted him and ran after him shouting, "Sir, you forgot your schmaltz!"

A Horse's Ass

Arrogant behavior is as old as human nature. "Wisdom is with those who receive counsel." (Proverbs 13:10.) While showing off is about showing off to others, arrogance is about showing off to yourself; you are deluding yourself and refusing to see the truth that is right before your eyes.

Many Polacks pride themselves as being excellent equestrians. As such, at a hospital picnic for staff and American visitors, all were invited to partake in a horse-riding jaunt in the forest. Only one visitor accepted the invitation disregarding the warnings of his colleagues that his equestrian skills were not on par with those of the hosts. Dr. R refused to heed their warnings, climbed up on his steed, smirked, and galloped off.

After about 30 minutes, a rider charged into the clearing announcing that, while riding full speed, "Dr. R's horse went to the right while Dr. R went to the left." Needless to say, Dr. R suffered a concussion and a broken wrist.

One of the unfortunate consequences of arrogance is that people who are guilty of possessing this trait often have no awareness of it and become defensive when confronted for grabbing more ground than they are entitled to. Needless to say, upon returning to the U.S., Dr. R consulted with a renowned hand surgeon fearing that the Polish team had lacked expertise. The surgeon's response was that Dr. R had received excellent care and should be grateful.

The Mirror

Edmund Burke 1729-1797

I look in the mirror
And what do I see?
A strange looking person
That cannot be me.
For I am much younger
And not nearly so fat
As that face in the mirror
I am looking at.
Oh, where are the mirrors
That I used to know
Like the ones which were
Made thirty years ago?
Now all things are changed
And I'm sure you'll agree
Mirrors are not as good
As they used to be.
So never be concerned,
If wrinkles appear
For one thing I've learned
Which is clear,
Should your complexion
Be less than perfection,
It is really the mirror
That needs correction!

No Regrets

Edith Piaf, the French chanteuse of the 1930s, sang the song, "No Regrets" about finding her new love. To love and be loved in return is the greatest thing you can ever learn (Nature Boy lyrics by Eden Ahbez). I, having no vocal talents but having loved and been loved throughout my life, can say with conviction: I have NO REGRETS.

One fact of life that we all need to acknowledge: regardless of our initial circumstances, is that we define our lives through the choices we make. Since life doesn't just happen, we need to recognize that our lives are defined by the decisions we make throughout our lives. Those decisions will determine the kind of life we will live. By the time we are 15 or 16-years old, each of us has almost total control over what we think, what we say and what we do as defined by the choices we make. Some choices we make on our own and others by simply going along with the choices of others. In either event, we get to choose. That doesn't mean that we are free from the consequences of our choices, or that sometimes those choices don't come from, or lead to, difficult circumstances—yet regardless, we always get to choose our next step. It's not what we do once in a while nor the conditions of our lives that count, but our consistent actions and choices that determine who we become, where we go in life, and how our destiny is determined.

Now, as I alternately glide and stumble through my 77th year, I am engaging in what gerontology professionals have termed life review (the process of looking back over one's own life, analyzing it, uncovering the hidden themes, and hopefully understanding its meaning). So far, this process has revealed to me that: (1.) I have consistently made good decisions; (2.) I am not humble in my convictions but I am sometimes curious about alternatives. Even though God gave us 2 ears and 1 mouth, (3.) I don't always listen twice as much as I speak; (4.) I truly believe that the only thing more dangerous than ignorance is arrogance; (5.) cooking can't kill you, but why take a chance; (6.) a great and humble man leans over to his shorter wife so that she can whisper the appropriate response into his ear; (7.) do no harm: smell as sweet as a rose and be not as cruel as its thorns; and, (8.) those who love and are loved are invincible BECAUSE I HAVE LIVED IT.

I have consistently made good choices throughout my life either because I had good instincts or was lucky enough to have had wise advisors and friends. The choices we face and the decisions we ultimately make become the foundation of who we are. Therefore, I am what I have chosen to be. Happiness is a choice you make . . . life isn't about what happens to you — it's about what you do about it. You can't change much about what happens in life, but you can change how you deal with adverse events. Unfortunately, we live in a time where intelligent people are being silenced so that stupid people won't be offended.

Make the most of what you have left and compensate for what you may have lost.

Endnotes

BACKOFF . . . Nazenti Store (Amazon.com)

Book Review . . . My Holocaust (Amir Gutfreund), Toby Press, 2006; reviewed by Annette Hintenach, (2018); Fordham University.

Barbara Crooker. *Weather Systems*. Les Fauves, 2018.

Marriage: Growing Older Together. Silverstone, Barbara and Hyman, K.H. *Growing Older Together*. Pantheon, New York, 1992.

Gibran, Khalili. ***The Prophet***. Alfred A. Knopf, New York 1923.

'Love is a Many Splendid Thing' . . . even unto illness: *The caregiver Wife*, Nieli Langer (2018). Educational Gerontology: 44:12, 741-742.

Book Review . . . Love and Sex; Are we ever too ***Old?*** (Niel Langer) Anne Wyatt-Brown. Educational Gerontology 2018; 44:10, 672-673.

Judith Viorst. About His Retirement in Suddenly Sixty and other shocks of later life. Simon & Schuster. New York, 2000. Reprinted by permission of Lescher & Lescher, Ltd. All rights reserved.

Nat King Cole . . . Nature Boy; Capitol Records, 1948.

Roulette Records (1963) ..Two Faces Have I Two Faces Have I (Nieli Langer) Educational Gerontology: 43:4 (2017): 173-174.

Jane Isay. *Walking on eggshells*. Anchor Books, 2008.

Preserving and eliciting memories. Nieli Langer (2018). Educational Gerontology: 44:2-3,81.

Book Review . . . The Lilith Summer (Hadley Irwin) The Feminist Press at CUNY, 1979. Reviewed by Danielle Jimenez, Fordham University 2018.

Erris Langer. A review of the movie, "On my way Out: The secret life of Nani and Popi. Educational Gerontology 44:2018 Special Issue: An Emerging Understanding of Grand Parenting for the 21% century: Guest Editor: Manoj Pardasani

Who moved my cheese? Adjusting to age-related changes (Nieli Langer) Educational Gerontology: 38:7 (2012):459-464.

Jill Mosley Langer and Mathew Love. The ties of later life: Aging siblings. Educational Gerontology 45:9(2019): 573-576

Printed in the United States
by Baker & Taylor Publisher Services